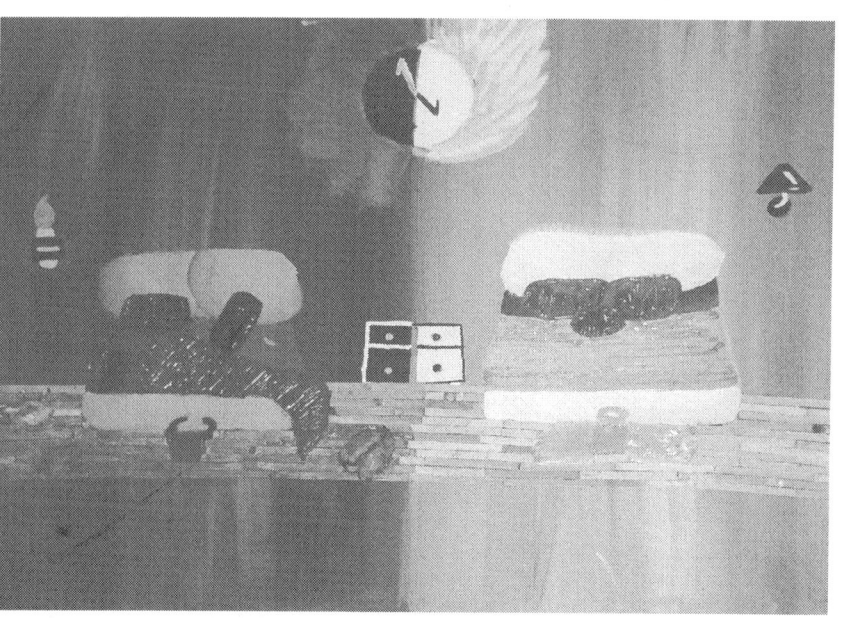

Confessions of a Pastor's Wife

Confessions of a Pastor's Wife

By Tomekia Moore

Copyright © 2025 by Tomkia Moore

All Rights Reserved.

Dedication:

To the Name above all names, the mighty and matchless Jesus Christ, thank You for Your visions, guidance, and everlasting love.

My Children:
Ivan, the "Get Right Mechanic"
Terri, find her at linktr.ee/coachterriamani
Terra, the Artist

My Mothers:
Mary Eason - Thank you for shaping me into the woman I am today.
Lorene King - My cherished granny mama.
Patricia Moore - My stepmom, who always greets me with a hearty "Howdy!"

My Dad:
Mr. Eugene Moore, Jr. - Your push and your continual pursuit of forgiveness have taught me the true meaning of humility.

Family Thanks:
Darius Robinson - My little BIG brother.
Doriselle & Orlando Robinson - My steadfast older siblings.
Susie Lockhart - Who has always been another mother to me.

My Friends and Supporters:
Corina Mapp, Ebony Constance, Dottia Taylor, Tashia Sledge, Tracell Smith, and "E" - Your support has been indispensable.

Thank You:

A special thank you to Ms. Ava Johnson and Ms. Sharyl Griggs, who both have been an indispensable support system for me. Your diligence and assistance in preparing materials for the editors were crucial in bringing this book to fruition. Your support not only facilitated the practical aspects of this project but also provided the encouragement needed to see it through. I am deeply grateful for your commitment.

Remember to recognize and appreciate the angels that the Lord places in your life—those who provide strong support systems that help you along your journey. Thank you both, for being one of my angels.

Special Apology:

To C. McGhee, I offer a sincere apology for any negative energy I may have caused. Your grace and understanding in the face of my mistakes are deeply appreciated. Your forgiveness has been a lesson in humility and kindness.

Final Thanks:

To everyone mentioned—and even those not listed by name—you have uplifted me and propelled me to levels that words can barely express. Thank you for being part of my journey, for every word of encouragement, and for the silent strength that has resonated so powerfully. Your support has been a beacon of hope and a testament to the power of community.

Preface

This book reaches out to the hearts of women married to pastors and ministers and to all who wish to glimpse behind the curtains of a pastor's home. It's a tribute to those who navigate the complexities of such a life, where every home is different and yet bound by common threads of faith, love, and, inevitably, human frailty.

In the pages of Scripture, we find guidance for these relationships. Genesis 2:24 outlines the sacred union of marriage: "Therefore, a man shall leave his father and his mother and hold fast to his wife, and they shall become one flesh." 1 Timothy 3:2 emphasizes fidelity among church elders, and Ephesians portrays marriage as a reflection of Christ's profound love for the church. These teachings remind us of the covenant shared between a pastor and his wife, akin to the vows they uphold in ministry.

I understand that being a pastor's wife comes with unique challenges that are often unseen and misunderstood by those outside the ministry. While I cannot share every detail of my own journey, my heart's desire is to offer a platform for other pastors' wives and women in general to voice their stories. Sharing is not just freeing; it is transformative.

If your heart is weighed down, if you feel silenced by the shadows of the ministry, know that you are not alone. This book is your invitation to speak, to share, and to start healing. Every story told in confidence will be received with open arms and respect. Your experiences are invaluable, and your voice can light the way for others in the quiet battles they face.

To share your story or just to connect, please reach out to me at pastorw395@gmail.com. Let's walk this journey together, in faith and in solidarity.

Chapter 1: How I Became a Pastor's Wife

"The Church in the Pasture" by Terra SC Wright

Perfection has never been my claim, nor my journey. Instead, my life has been a testament to how imperfections, embraced and transformed by grace, can lead to unexpected destinies. At sixteen, life handed me a significant challenge—I became pregnant with my boyfriend, Jim. By seventeen, I was a young mother, navigating the complexities of parenthood with a baby on my hip and high school books in my backpack. At twenty-one, after overcoming alcoholism and leaving behind dreams of pediatric medicine due to a traumatic experience, I was deep into a new relationship with Diego, a friend from middle school, and pursuing an associate's degree in technology repair.

Life then was a daily struggle for survival and stability. I remember the cold mornings at bus stops, clutching a baby carrier and school supplies, barely scraping together enough money for bus fare. Often, I would exchange food stamps for cash just to ensure we could get by. The responsibility of raising my son was split between my mother—whom he affectionately called Nana—and his father's mother, Granny, requiring long treks through the darkness after my night classes.

The wisdom of my parents, despite their divorce, served as my guiding light during these turbulent times. My father emphasized the essentials: education, a husband, and a stable home. My mother bolstered these lessons with her relentless encouragement to "keep pushing" and "stay focused and get it done." Their advice was the bedrock upon which I tried to build my life, even as I occasionally strayed from the path they had envisioned for me.

My marriage to Diego, however, began to disintegrate within two years. It was during this time that we encountered Paul at church, where he served as our Christian Education teacher. His classes, filled with discussions on Christian principles, became a refuge for me. Diego, increasingly absorbed by video games and emotionally distant, contrasted sharply with Paul, who provided the understanding and engagement I craved. This emotional connection eventually led to an affair and a subsequent pregnancy—a real-life echo of the biblical tale of David and Bathsheba, where sin compounded by attempts to conceal it only led to greater pain and eventual public scandal.

Despite the messy complexity of teenage pregnancy, alcoholism, and infidelity, God's presence in my life felt unwavering. His grace was a profound force, shaping my spirit and character, preparing me for a role I never imagined—serving alongside a man of God as his wife. This journey underscores the truth that God can use anyone, regardless of their past. If you are wrestling with regrets or burdened by past choices, remember you are not alone. God's grace is boundless, capable of transforming our deepest flaws into vessels of beauty and purpose.

The path to ministry is seldom straightforward; it often meanders through valleys of mistakes and over mountains of regret. Yet, every step, even the missteps, is orchestrated as part of God's greater plan. Your past does not disqualify you from His work; it often prepares you uniquely to help others on similar paths. Paul and I went on to welcome our second child and navigated through various churches until he found a steady ministry position an hour away from our home.

Embrace your journey, for it is uniquely yours, and it is replete with unseen beauty and potential for redemption.

Chapter 2: The Cost of Sharing Your Pastor-Husband

"The Heart of it All" by Terra SC Wright

Initially, the idea of being a pastor's wife filled me with excitement. I envisioned myself serving alongside my husband, participating in every facet of church life—from morning worship and evening prayers to choir rehearsals and community dinners. The prospect of opening doors, both literally and figuratively, for God's parishioners thrilled me. My heart soared at the thought of giving back, standing by my husband as we served together.

However, the reality of "sharing" my husband with the congregation was far different from what I had imagined. It wasn't just about his time; it was about the emotional toll it took on our family. His days were consumed by his regular 9-5 job, funerals, counseling sessions, and seemingly endless church meetings. Emergencies took precedence, and family time was often the first sacrifice.

I tried to find my own role within the church. Despite my eagerness, my attempts were met with resistance—whether it was criticism of my singing in the choir or being shut out of counseling sessions I wished to attend. Even simple acts of service like cleaning the church or caring for the grounds were frowned upon by Paul. It seemed my place was to be seen and not heard, an arrangement that chafed against my desire to actively serve.

Yet, I carved out a niche by nurturing relationships within the church community. Our home was an hour from the church, but I used this distance to deepen connections. I visited church members, learning about their lives, their families, and even their livestock. The rural charm of our congregation, with their pastures and well water, endeared them to me. The church secretary, an older lady who became a dear friend and mentor, crafted bespoke garments for me and offered sage advice that helped me navigate the storms brewing within our church walls.

Despite these connections, the emotional distance from my husband grew. Special occasions were overlooked, swallowed by his pastoral duties. Once, I watched, heartbroken from our bathroom window as he returned from a breakfast with a deacon on a day that should have been ours to celebrate together. The loneliness of being a "single married woman" caring for our two daughters, both managing juvenile diabetes, and being separated from my first born, whose father decided to come back into his life, all weighed heavily on me.

The challenge of sharing my husband wasn't just about managing time; it was about juggling emotional availability, priorities, and our family's needs. When every church crisis overshadowed our personal lives, it created wounds difficult to heal, teaching me resilience in solitude and the true cost of service in a pastoral family.

Chapter 3: The Pressure on a Pastor's Kid

"Kids Toys & Trinkets" by Terra SC Wright

From the outside, people see the perfect family photos—the pastor, the first lady, and their children, all smiling as if they've stepped out of a picture-perfect life. Onlookers say, *Awww, what a happy family!* And to some extent, we were. But beneath the polished Sunday morning smiles lay pressures, expectations, and wounds that no one outside the home could see.

My girls were wonderful, always well-behaved, involved in school, and busy with activities. As their mother and their teacher, I made sure their schedules were full—partly for their benefit but also to maintain their image as pastor's kids (PKs). In the eyes of the church, they had to be perfect. Their hair had to be neatly styled, their clothes pristine, their behavior beyond reproach. Church wasn't just a place of worship for them—it was a stage where they had to play the role of the "ideal pastor's children."

My son, however, experienced a different kind of pressure. He lived with his father from the age of eleven to twenty-one, a decision I thought would protect him from the struggles in my marriage. I convinced myself that shielding him from the dysfunction would be better than exposing him to it. But distance didn't protect him—it left a wound. He felt my absence and that weighed on him in ways I didn't fully understand at the time.

Meanwhile, my daughters had a front-row seat to the realities of our home life. They bore witness to the endless arguments, the nights filled with shouting between me and Paul, the tension that never seemed to dissipate. Sleep was often interrupted by raised voices, and they were forced to navigate a home where love was one-sided and respect was conditional. They may not have fully understood what was happening at the time, but as they grew, their questions became harder to answer.

"Mommy, why is Daddy so mean to you?"

It was in those moments, as their small hands wiped my tears, that I realized just how much they understood. I had spent so much time protecting them from the world outside that I hadn't realized they were quietly suffering inside our home. They were too young to carry that kind of burden, but it was placed on them nonetheless.

One particular memory still stings. My daughter had missed a school field trip due to her diabetes, so their father and I planned a make-up trip to Nashville. It was meant to be a fun, relaxing getaway—just a simple overnight trip. But instead, it turned into a nightmare.

We arrived at the hotel, exhausted from the drive, only for him to declare that the room wasn't good enough. Without hesitation, he demanded a refund, reloaded the car, and decided we were leaving. The girls were hungry, their blood sugar was dropping, and they couldn't understand why we were being forced back into the car. But we left anyway, arguing the entire drive home. We ate in the car, the joy of the trip completely stolen. Moments that should have been about family and love were instead overshadowed by pride and control.

Being a PK came with pressures the girls didn't fully comprehend until they were older. They were expected to be perfect, to sit still in church, to smile even when they were tired. They had to be polite and respectful and always say "Yes, ma'am" or "Yes, sir." If they ever acted up, I had my own silent way of correcting them—a look, a quiet countdown—and they knew better than to test me beyond that.

As they grew, they not only questioned the way I raised them but also the actions of their father. The more they studied God's Word, the more they saw the contradictions between what was preached in the pulpit and what was practiced at home. Their father's authority had always been absolute, but they started to see beyond the title of "pastor." They saw his actions, his treatment of me, and the emotional turmoil it caused.

My son, too, was deeply affected. He had always prayed for a little sister, and when he finally got one, it wasn't in the way he had expected. He was forced to navigate the complexities of our broken family, and it hardened him in ways I wish it hadn't.

The truth is, your children *do* suffer from your mistakes, your disobedience, and your brokenness. I made choices that I thought were best at the time, but looking back, I see the ripples they created in my children's lives.

I remarried out of guilt and shame, believing that I could fix the mistakes of my past. I thought that by moving forward, by marrying the father of my daughters, I could erase the pain of infidelity and broken vows. But I only created a bigger mess. For one solid year, everything seemed beautiful. And then for thirteen more years, life was a slow-burning hell.

From the outside, everything looked great. He was an excellent provider. He made sure we had what we needed. But provision without love is empty. The marriage became a performance—a never-ending game of "show and tell." I kept trying to prove my love, to be the perfect wife, to show that we were a strong pastoral family. But no matter what I did, it was never enough.

And my son? He was the outsider in his own home. My husband never saw him as part of the family. To him, my son was the wedge, the bad apple, the child that didn't belong. No matter how hard I tried to make my husband love him, it never happened.

Looking back, I realize how much my children endured because of *my* choices—choices I made thinking I was doing the right thing. But God's love is bigger than our mistakes. It's His grace that carried us through.

I've learned that as much as we want to protect our children, our brokenness affects them whether we intend for it to or not. But I also know that no matter how deep the wounds, God is still the healer. Despite everything, my children are strong, resilient, and courageous. And through it all, we have learned that no title, no position, and no outward appearance will ever matter more than the truth.

Chapter 4: The Weight of Secrets

"Just Tutting Around, All Eyes on Me" By: Terra S.C. Wright

Being a pastor's wife entails navigating a world filled with secrets—secrets that belong to me, to my husband, and to the entire congregation. The late-night calls, the early morning visits, and the never-ending church politics form the backdrop of our lives. "Holy Sally" isn't always holy, and "Deacon Do-Right" might just have more skeletons in his closet than one could imagine.

I quickly learned that the image of a happy, perfect family is often just that—an image. Behind the smiles and the Sunday best, there are struggles, whispered confessions, and hidden pains. As the pastor's wife, you become the keeper of these secrets, which can lead to deep isolation and even depression. Your every move, every choice scrutinized—not just by your husband, but by the entire community.

Maintaining the facade of a perfect life is exhausting. You have to look the part—your appearance can't falter, or it reflects poorly on your husband. The better you look and the wider your smile, the more people assume your life is flawless. But the reality is, carrying the burdens of an entire congregation is crushing.

Through the years, I realized that many of the calls to our home weren't just requests for prayer or help during family crises. There were other, often unspoken needs and intentions. As the first lady, it was expected that I would endure it all and remain a paragon of virtue. But what really defines a "good woman"? Is she simply one who stands by her man, no matter what? Is she one who guards every secret, even when it starts eating away at her soul?

The relationship I developed with the church secretary, who also doubled as my private seamstress, became one of my most treasured sanctuaries. Over brunch or during fitting sessions, we would share stories and laughter, providing a much-needed respite from the weight of our roles. She taught me the true meaning of confidentiality and the delicate balance of being a confidante.

One incident, however, changed everything—a slip of the tongue by someone my husband trusted. It unleashed a torrent of consequences that reshaped our lives dramatically. That day, I learned the true power of secrets and the irreversible impact they can have.

Reflecting on these experiences, I've come to understand the importance of seeking counsel and not just keeping to ourselves. I learned from my husband what not to do—gossip can destroy lives. Instead, I chose to pray for those around me, to be a counselor, fostering deep and lasting relationships that have enriched my life far beyond the church walls.

This chapter taught me that secrets can be burdensome, but they can also teach us valuable lessons about trust, discretion, and the profound impact of our words and actions. As a pastor's wife, these experiences have sculpted me into someone who not only carries secrets but also carries the wisdom to handle them with care.

Chapter 5: The Power of Fasting and Prayer

"Peace in the Valley" By: Terra S.C. Wright

Marriage, a divine covenant blessed by God, demands more than mere human wisdom; it requires divine intervention, especially when it falters. The Bible teaches that no one should come between spouses and that couples should seek God's wisdom above all. In today's world, where societal norms often conflict with divine instructions, it becomes even more crucial to adhere to these teachings, especially when navigating the complexities of human relationships and societal decay.

During my marriage, which increasingly felt devoid of love and filled only with sacrifice, I relied heavily on fasting and prayer. These practices helped me discern true needs from deceptions within and outside the church community, as we are commanded to help the needy but also to be wise and discerning.

My health began to reflect the turmoil within my marriage. Stress manifested physically; frequent hospital visits became my escape from the pain at home. The nadir of my struggles came when doctors thought they found a tumor in my brain at the base of my spine, preparing me for immediate brain surgery that turned out to be unnecessary due to a misdiagnosis. This terrifying experience brought my husband to my side in prayer, marking a rare moment of genuine connection that had become scarce in our relationship.

This ordeal taught me the undeniable power of prayer and the peace that comes from complete reliance on God. During my hospital stay, I found solace in the care of familiar faces and managed to focus on my studies, turning a time of potential despair into one of productivity and spiritual growth. This time reinforced the importance of self-advocacy in healthcare, a crucial lesson I passed on to my daughters.

The Bible recounts in Matthew 17 how the disciples failed to cast out a demon due to their lack of faith. Like them, I learned that profound faith and persistent prayer are potent tools against life's adversities. My faith deepened during my ordeal, teaching me to listen for God's subtle communications, which often guided me through other challenges, such as the night I was locked out of our home with my children. In that moment, a quiet reminder of an open kitchen window from God led to a simple yet profound solution.

Isaiah 58 and Matthew 6 highlight the transformative power of fasting, not as a public display of piety but as a private communion with God. These practices broke the bonds weighing me down, eventually leading to a clear indication from God that it was time to leave my troubled marriage. With nothing but faith guiding me, I found that God provided for me and my children, just as He promises to deliver those who call on Him in times of trouble.

Chapter 6: A Pastor's Wife's Guide - Do' & Don'ts

"Sun & Flowers" By: Terra S.C. Wright

As a pastor's wife, understanding the unique challenges and blessings of this role is crucial. Below are some guiding principles, drawn from personal experience and biblical wisdom, to navigate this path with grace and strength. Make sure you **speak the truth in love.**

Do's:

- **Maintain Your Identity:** Keep a strong personal relationship with God independent of your spouse. Develop your own spiritual disciplines and prayer life.
- **Pursue Personal Goals:** Continue striving towards your personal ambitions and maintain hobbies and interests outside the church.
- **Set Boundaries:** It's essential to establish clear boundaries for family and marriage time. Protect these times from non-emergency church matters.
- **Seek Support:** Find a counselor outside your church network for unbiased advice. Build a support network that includes other pastors' wives seeking answers through support and maintain old friendships.
- **Care for Yourself:** Prioritize your mental and emotional health with regular self-care activities. Don't ignore signs of emotional exhaustion or depression.

Don'ts:

- **Avoid Perfectionism:** Accept your imperfections and understand that you don't have to be perfect to be effective and loved.
- **Watch for Red Flags:** Be aware of controlling behaviors or any signs of emotional or spiritual abuse. Set firm boundaries and seek help if mistreated.
- **Keep Boundaries Firm:** Protect your personal time and space. Ensure that the church does not consume every aspect of your family life.
- **Avoid Gossip:** Stay clear of church politics and gossip. Use discretion in handling sensitive information and redirect conversations towards more constructive topics.
- **Embrace Your Calling:** Remember, being a pastor's wife is about being true to yourself and using your unique gifts to support and nurture others. Don't feel confined by your husband's role.

Personal Reflection:

From the onset, know what you stand for and what you won't tolerate. If you find yourself in a situation where your values are compromised, have the courage to walk away gracefully. Remember, all people are created in God's image, but not all behaviors align with His will. It's okay to leave a situation where you feel disrespected or devalued.

Spiritual Insight:

Remember that your worth isn't determined by your husband's position or by the perfection of your actions. God uses all of us, flaws and all, for His glory. If you find yourself struggling, reach out for help—you don't have to bear your burdens alone.

Conclusion:

Navigating the life of a pastor's wife demands a delicate balance of grace, resilience, and personal strength. By adhering to these guidelines, you can sustain a fulfilling life while supporting your spouse's ministry. Remember, always give yourself grace as you journey through this unique role, recognizing that your authentic self is your greatest gift to both your family and your congregation.

Reflecting on my years in a marriage that was often more sacrificial than sanctifying, I am grateful for the personal growth it spurred. I've come to cherish the peace that accompanies life's quiet moments and the profound joy of truly loving someone—not despite their flaws, but because of them.

The day I felt called to leave was marked by a surreal, divine encounter. For years, I allowed my desires to steer me into a marriage more guided by flesh than by spirit. However, in its dissolution, I was determined not to repeat those mistakes. I prayed fervently, journaled relentlessly, and grappled with the challenges within our families. The path to leaving was neither easy nor without its own set of traumas.

Yet, there came a morning when everything shifted. Awakening to a profound sense of clarity, as if directly spoken to by God, I sat on the edge of my bed with the morning light filtering through the curtains. A voice deep within my soul said clearly, "You're free to go." It was not a voice of anger or impulse, but one of liberation and peace.

The voice was so distinct, so commanding, that I heard it twice, in two different parts of my house—and I know there was no one else there but me. Both times, the message was unequivocal: "You are free to go." With that affirmation, I gathered my things and my girls—my son had already been removed from the situation. I kissed my husband goodbye, told him I loved him, and from that day, I have not looked back. Homeless, happy, and terrified, I embarked on a new journey. Eventually, I moved my family into a home, my divorce was finalized 14 years ago, I've increased my education, skills and knowledge during that time and all of my children have developed into beautiful, talented, productive adults who each have their own loving characteristics.

By sharing my story, I aim to reassure those in similar circumstances that they are not alone. Your path may be fraught with difficulties, but it is also lined with opportunities for profound personal growth and spiritual enlightenment. Listen closely for that quiet voice within, the one that guides you toward your truth, and trust that when you walk in faith, you truly never walk alone.

Family Photos:

My son as a teenager

My son & me (at age 20)

Me as First lady

My daughters & me

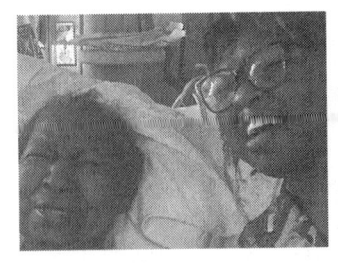

Me & Mom

My Dad

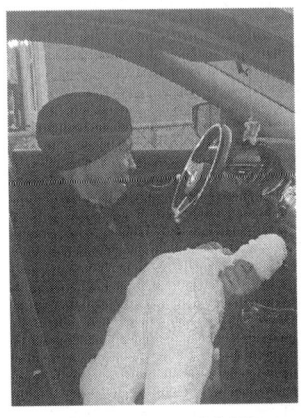

Mom & great grandchild

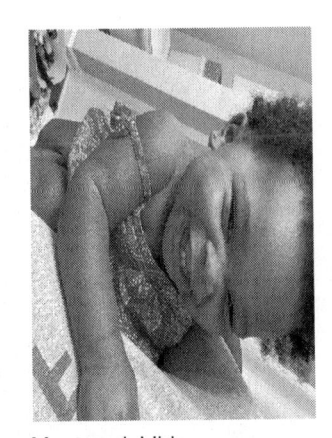

My grandchild

Me & My daughters

Me & my siblings

Made in the USA
Columbia, SC
06 May 2025